Little Laureates

Eastern England

Edited by Mark Richardson

YoungWriters

First published in Great Britain in 2007 by:
Young Writers
Remus House
Coltsfoot Drive
Peterborough
PE2 9JX
Telephone: 01733 890066
Website: www.youngwriters.co.uk

SB ISBN 978-1 84431 128 6

Foreword

Young Writers was established in 1991 and has been passionately devoted to the promotion of reading and writing in children and young adults ever since. The quest continues today. Young Writers remains as committed to the nurturing of poetic and literary talent as ever.

This year's Young Writers competition has proven as vibrant and dynamic as ever and we are delighted to present a showcase of the best poetry from across the UK and in some cases overseas. Each poem has been selected from a wealth of *Little Laureates* entries before ultimately being published in this, our sixteenth primary school poetry series.

Once again, we have been supremely impressed by the overall quality of the entries we have received. The imagination, energy and creativity which has gone into each young writer's entry made choosing the poems a challenging and often difficult but ultimately hugely rewarding task - the general high standard of the work submitted ensured this opportunity to bring their poetry to a larger appreciative audience.

We sincerely hope you are pleased with this final collection and that you will enjoy *Little Laureates Eastern England* for many years to come.

Contents

The Poems

Slithery Snake

Sliding, slithering,
Spying, scary,
Hissing, spooky,
Mysterious, secret,
Small but thin,
Biting,

Non-boned snake.

Ronnie Bowyer (9)
Great Clacton CE Junior School, Clacton-on-Sea

Fireworks

Colours, colours and more sparkling colours,
Bang, bang, bang,
Sizzle, sizzle, pop,
Purple, green, red,
Sizzle, sizzle, pop,
Fireworks, fireworks, your spectacular colours,
Way up high the colours look like gems,
Sizzle, sizzle, pop.

Dani Muir (10)
Great Clacton CE Junior School, Clacton-on-Sea

Spectacular Spring!

Spring is here, hooray, hooray!
The lambs are out in the fields to play,
The days are now getting longer as the
Clocks have sprung forward,
I can't wait until spring!

Daffodils, bright and yellow stand tall,
Tulips, all colours, grow against the wall,
Crocuses and snowdrops starting to bloom,
I can't wait until spring!

The shops are full of Easter eggs,
All different shapes and sizes,
Colourful and bright and filled with surprises,
I can't wait until spring!

Family's have the chance to get together,
Great fun is had by all,
Parties, games and Easter egg hunts,
I can't wait until spring!

Charlotte Harvey (10)
Great Clacton CE Junior School, Clacton-on-Sea

My Family

My sister's name is Hayley,
She is tall and cool,
She may be very annoying,
But she is beautiful most of all.

My mum's name is Mandy,
She does everything for me,
She takes me here and there,
This is very handy.

My dad's name is Tom,
He works very hard,
He drinks loads of beer
And my cousin calls him Pom.

Emily May Nikolson (10)
Great Clacton CE Junior School, Clacton-on-Sea

Chocolate

Chocolate, chocolate,
In my tummy,
Yummy, yummy,
Melting in my mouth,
Sometimes dark,
Sometimes light,
Sometimes even white,
All smooth and soft,
Galaxy and Dairy,
Favourites, Mars and even Maltesers,
Chocolate is the best,
Better than the rest.

Megan Barnard (9)
Great Clacton CE Junior School, Clacton-on-Sea

My Dad

My dad cares,
My dad shares,
My dad is always there,
He loves football and more sports,
But I still don't care because I love him!
He's my dad!
Even though he can be mad,
He always falls asleep,
I still don't care,
I love him!
My dad will always care,
My dad will always share,
My dad will always be there.

Maria Edwards (10)
Great Clacton CE Junior School, Clacton-on-Sea

Boring

B oring, I say boring!
O ut with my mum and sisters,
R ight to the shops we go,
I n one and out, then in another,
N o! No more please!
G reat, time to go home at last!

Scott Fisher (9)
Great Clacton CE Junior School, Clacton-on-Sea

The Weather

Raindrops patter on the ground,
Snow is falling all around,
Then comes thunder, lightning too,
The sun is trying to break through.

All the creatures are running home,
All that is left is a garden gnome,
One of the ditches is overflowing,
The wind is now violently blowing.

Then after a while the sun breaks through,
A rainbow appears red, yellow and blue,
The last raindrop falls to the ground,
Then it stops, not another sound.

Jessica Connor (10)
Great Clacton CE Junior School, Clacton-on-Sea

Weather

Weather is good,
Weather is bad,
When I'm happy,
Or when I'm sad,
When the rain comes falling down,
My face drops, I start to frown,
But when the sun comes out to shine,
My face changes with a new design.

Shannon Smith (10)
Great Clacton CE Junior School, Clacton-on-Sea

Football

Football is my favourite game,
Cheeky Charlie is my name,
My mum is a big Spurs fan,
But I won't play at White Hart Lane,
My favourite team are all in blue
And winning is what they can do,
The kings of Stamford Bridge they're called,
John Terry and co, they all rule,
Chelsea, Chelsea is their name
And playing for them is my aim.

Charlie Kenny (9)
Great Clacton CE Junior School, Clacton-on-Sea

Once In A Garden

Once in a spring garden,
As I was walking by,
A little tiny robin,
Went fluttering gently by.

Once in a summer garden,
As I went skipping by,
That same little robin,
Glided gently through the sky.

Once in an autumn garden,
As I went running by,
That cute little robin,
In the wind it tried to fly.

Once in a winter garden,
As snow was drifting by,
The lovely little robin,
Was nestling in the dry.

Lauren Coppin (10)
Great Clacton CE Junior School, Clacton-on-Sea

Nightmare

The lights go out and night is here,
Times of darkness and times of fear,
Fire-breathing dragons in their lair,
Is it real or just a nightmare?

Witches on brooms up high in the skies,
Out of his coffin Dracula flies,
Frankenstein's up and wanting to scare,
Is it real or just a nightmare?

Ghosts and phantoms all start to moan,
Ghouls and goblins join in and groan,
Fighting all these things that scare,
Was it real or just a nightmare?

Ben Castle (9)
Great Clacton CE Junior School, Clacton-on-Sea

Dreams! Dreams! Dreams!

It's 8 o'clock and it's time for bed,
It's finally time to rest my head,
My teeth are brushed and my PJs are on,
After a kiss goodnight Mum is gone,
I enter a world of magical things,
Dragons, giants and horses with wings,
I fly in the air with pigs all around,
They grunt and they sing - what an awful sound,
I swim in the sea with a fluffy bear,
I ride on a sea horse, an underground fair,
Dreams are wonderful, you can be anyone,
A world of adventure, a night of fun!

Scott Hazell (9)
Great Clacton CE Junior School, Clacton-on-Sea

Living In Hope

I'm tired, hungry and cold
And still I'm waiting to be sold,
I can't hang on much longer 'cause I'm getting very old.

No person will ever want me,
'Cause I'm not their cup of tea,
I'm not a pretty sight to see.

I sit in a cage day and night,
Watching the birds in flight
And I try and hide myself from sight.

My fur is matted
And my brain is scattered,
But that doesn't bother me.

I used to have an owner, but he left me when he died,
I sat by day and howled, and by night I cried and cried,
I just want a home and to be loved by someone like you,
Two arms to cuddle, a heart that's kind and a
Smiling face will do.

My name is Lucky
And I'm a bit mucky,
But I'm still waiting for a person like you.

Hannah Clark (10)
Great Clacton CE Junior School, Clacton-on-Sea

How Do Birds Fly?

How do birds fly
So high in the sky?
They soar like an eagle,
They are as fast as a falcon.

Flying like a bird,
So high in the sky,
Looking down on the world,
With a gleam in their eye.

They look for food
And objects that are shiny,
Maybe a lost key,
That can be tiny.

As they soar in the sky,
Looking for prey to take back to the nests,
We will always wonder; how do birds fly?

Andrew Jeffrey (10)
Great Clacton CE Junior School, Clacton-on-Sea

Gymnastics

G ymnastics are fantastic,
Y ou're as flexible as a caterpillar,
M any people join the fun,
N o one sits there on their bum,
A lways having the best time ever,
S plits, handstands even backflips,
T aking your time to make the skills better,
I nstead of adults being embarrassed,
C hildren take their hands and join in,
S o many people have loads of fun.

Heather Madge (10)
Great Clacton CE Junior School, Clacton-on-Sea

River Poem

The river flows down the stream,
The sun shines on it with its red-hot beam,
It runs into the sea,
Children swim in it with glee,
You're so blue and clear,
When you twinkle you're saying I'm here,
The day is all done,
The sun has gone down,
You're no longer around,
As I turn to go home, I say goodbye,
You twinkle at me for the very last time.

Abbey Priestley (9)
Great Clacton CE Junior School, Clacton-on-Sea

Jess

I have a little kitten, her name is Jess,
She is black and white and likes to make a mess!

She licks me and it tickles, she purrs when she is asleep,
When she plays, she likes to jump and leap.

I love my little kitten, I'm glad I called her Jess,
I love to snuggle next to her,
But I don't' like it when she makes a mess!

Charly Muir (9)
Great Clacton CE Junior School, Clacton-on-Sea

The Nile

The beautiful Nile,
Runs for more than three miles,
Every year it has a flood,
Leaving behind a layer of mud,
So now the people
Can grow their food,
Sometimes they do the work
In the nude,
Walking along in single file,
Is a line of crocodile,
Luxor, Libya, Sahara and Cairo,
All of the countries,
All four cities can see the Nile's flow.

Charlotte Hooker (10)
Great Clacton CE Junior School, Clacton-on-Sea

My Illness

I had an operation then I got quite sick,
I went in an ambulance to another hospital quick.

The doctors gave me medicine to make me go to sleep,
I was attached to many machines, they had a very loud beep.

My organs inside were failing, Mummy was told that I could die,
They gave me lots of medicine, my mummy started to cry.

I had tubes and needles put into my skin,
It was through there that the medicine went in.

After about a week, I started to get better,
All my friends from school sent me presents, cards and letters.

When I was woken from my long, long sleep,
I couldn't move my arms or legs and all I did was weep.

Because when I was sleeping my muscles wasted away,
No longer could I run and jump or go outside to play.

I had to learn all over again, to eat and drink and walk,
I felt like a little baby, all I could do was talk.

I was in hospital for a long time, I had to have physio,
Now I am much stronger, although I have a way to go.

Now my legs are weak and I cannot walk far,
I get pushed in my wheelchair or go out in the car.

I like to go to school with my friends,
I've just started to play in the playground again.

One day I hope my legs get better so I can run and jump and skip,
Sometimes I try to do it but I just fall down or trip.

I will keep on trying to make my little legs grow strong,
I am not going to give up, I will prove this illness wrong!

Kirstie-Jade Legate (9)
Great Clacton CE Junior School, Clacton-on-Sea

Brilliant, Brilliant Arsenal

Arsenal are good, Arsenal are great,
We will win the league in 2008.

In defence we have Toure,
When he has the ball,
The crowd shout hooray,
Get it out to them all.

In midfield we have Walcott,
He scored in the final,
It's really a shame,
It's the only goal he's got.

Up front we have van Persie, Adebayor and Henry,
They all know where the goal should be,
So there's my team - nicknamed The Gunners,
I don't like any of the others,
At the end of the game,
They will have the ball,
That's why I support,
Brilliant, brilliant Arsenal!

Jack Johnson (10)
Great Clacton CE Junior School, Clacton-on-Sea

The Air

The air is cold and breezy,
The air is like the tops of the trees,
All freezing cold.

The air is like the loving person in the garden,
The air is our lifestyle place and
I dance in the air.

Georgia Jean Caskey (9)
Great Clacton CE Junior School, Clacton-on-Sea

School Time

When I was young
And went to school,
Work wasn't fun
And football was cool.

I sat inside,
Didn't pay attention,
Couldn't do my work,
So I got a detention!

Playtime arrived,
The sun was shining,
It was sweating hot,
The light was blinding.

I swapped my cards,
With my friends,
I hoped this playtime,
Never ends.

The bell soon rang,
Playtime was over,
Back to class
And spoke to Lola.

All lesson I chattered,
I got in real big trouble,
My stupid detention
Turned into double!

Lunchtime arrives,
Got pushed in the queue,
Split my head open,
At half-past two.

When I was young,
I didn't have a care,
Now that I'm older,
I live in despair!

Ryan Scott (9)
Great Clacton CE Junior School, Clacton-on-Sea

Spring

Spring is a fantastic time,
Lambs start leaping in the wonderful sun,
Baby chicks and a baby son!
Daffodils, apples and limes,
They are my favourite things at springtime!

The sun is as bright as bright can be,
Lambs are bouncy balls,
As my mum calls,
I come skipping in for tea,
They are my favourite things in springtime!

There are rows of rainbow flowers,
With the greenest stems you'd ever see,
The leaves start growing back on the old oak tree,
With all the colours, it looks like flowers,
They are my favourite things in springtime!

Zena Bresnan (8)
Great Clacton CE Junior School, Clacton-on-Sea

Chickens Are Great!

Chickens, chickens, chickens,
They are really great,
When I have dinner,
I eat them on a plate,
My mum cooks them quickly,
So I don't have to wait,
Chickens, chickens, chickens,
They are really great.

Archie Smith (10)
Great Clacton CE Junior School, Clacton-on-Sea

Weather

Good weather, bad weather,
That changes all the time,
Sometimes it rains,
Sometimes it's sunshine.

It's cold in autumn,
Windy too,
When it rains,
You'll get wet through.

Winter is the coldest,
With snow and ice,
I like to slip and slide,
It is very nice.

Spring is warm,
But plenty of April showers,
I splash in puddles,
Sometimes for hours.

Summer is very hot,
With lots of sun,
I play in paddling pools,
Having lots of fun.

George Johnson (8)
Great Clacton CE Junior School, Clacton-on-Sea

The Springtime Pond

One day I went for a walk,
Round the radiant springtime pond,
It was gleaming with brightness,
As I glared at it joyfully,
I watched the fish jump out with happiness,
That is the best thing about spring.

In a joyful mood,
I fed the fish,
They looked nourished as I did so,
Some were a rainbow of colours,
They were as scaly as a snake,
That is the best thing about spring.

I looked around and saw some daffodils,
They were the golden sun,
The bluebells were beautiful,
The buttercups were perfect,
I walked home in a brilliant mood,
That is the best thing about spring.

Cem Lacin (9)
Great Clacton CE Junior School, Clacton-on-Sea

The Springtime Pond

In the golden springtime pond,
There shone down the magnificent sun,
It glowed as beautiful as the sky,
It was so beautiful,
It was so colourful,
It was so bright.

The rosy red lips were decorating the springtime pond,
So was the golden sun,
All the little gnomes looked like towers,
So did the ducks,
The frogs were trying to swim,
While all the baby fish were being born.

Lauren Ince (9)
Great Clacton CE Junior School, Clacton-on-Sea

Easter

E aster is cool, Easter is fun, Easter is great for everyone,
A ngels are small and not very tall,
S urprises with Easter eggs will come to all,
T he eggs will show you of new life,
E aster eggs are melting in your mouth,
R abbits are fun, rabbits are cool but they're little devils.

Georgia Wilkins (10)
Great Clacton CE Junior School, Clacton-on-Sea

The Lovely Vase

For sale, a lovely vase,
In good condition
And helpful to put flowers in,
There are some
Roses in it as well.

There are some shields,
Swords and loads of other
Weapons for sale,
Some lovely sets
Of plates and glasses for sale.

Louise Harris (10)
Great Clacton CE Junior School, Clacton-on-Sea

Nature

Whispering trees,
Leaves that catch the sunlight,
Long walks in the country,
Morning dew.

Birds singing in the trees,
Busy nest-building,
Slugs slither silently,
Swifts swoop softly.

Ants like soldiers march to work,
Bees buzz brightly on the flower petals,
Luscious ladybirds land elegantly,
Sly spiders watch eagerly for lunch.

Beautiful butterflies burst with bright colours,
Creepy caterpillars crawl across the juicy leaves,
Graceful grasshoppers hop happily,
Flies swoop annoyingly like a Doodlebug from World War II.

Dandelions droop delicately,
Sunflowers sunbathe,
Bluebells brighten up the garden,
Green grass grows.

Emily Luxford (10)
Great Clacton CE Junior School, Clacton-on-Sea

God's Creation

God made a creation,
Specially for me,
He made a little girl,
As beautiful as can be.

Chloe Morris (9)
Great Clacton CE Junior School, Clacton-on-Sea

Anger

Anger reminds you of dark colours and dark things
Like hot red fire and dark gloomy places,
Like in the forest at night and in the woods,
Sometimes anger gets you down and
You need cheering up but you don't cheer up
Because you're angry, sad or upset,
But when you're angry, sad or upset, just try and
Cheer up!

Poppy Chapman-Dasent (10)
Park Junior School, Wellingborough

Hunger

Hunger is blue like heavy, hailing rain,
It smells like long-time mouldy garbage,
It sounds like a rumbling tummy going mad,
It feels like red, wobbling strawberry jelly on a plate,
It tastes like horrid smelly diapers,
It looks like green, sloppy sick,
It reminds me of the dead coming back to life.

Elliot Wilson (8)
Park Junior School, Wellingborough

Laughter

Laughter is orange like the sun on a sunny day,
It sounds like happiness on a summer holiday,
It tastes like a multicoloured sundae with loads of chocolate sauce,
It smells like flowers in a flower bed,
It looks like the bright sun,
It feels like bright pink rose petals,
It reminds me of a smile from my baby sister.

Lauren Martin (8)
Park Junior School, Wellingborough

Love

Love is as red as a love heart in the sky,
It looks like an enchanted red balloon,
It smells like a fresh, clean strawberry,
It tastes like home-made hot chocolate,
It sounds like soft music,
It feels like warm lava,
It reminds me of sweets from a Valentine's card.

Kalen Lennox (8)
Park Junior School, Wellingborough

Fear

Fear is green like the green, growing grass,
It looks like a green, ghouly ghost,
It sounds like a screaming girl.

It feels like a dead body inside a tomb,
It smells like diesel coming out of a garbage truck,
It tastes like my grandad's old smelly socks,
It reminds me of a murder in the middle of a graveyard
At 12.00 at night.

Olivia Keane (8)
Park Junior School, Wellingborough

Hunger

Hunger is yellow like the big bright sun,
It looks like someone feeling sick without any food,
It sounds like rumbling garbage,
It tastes like mushy, dirty, dark garbage,
It smells like the dark blue salty sea,
It feels like the gigantic rumbling earth,
It reminds me of when I was not allowed
Any beautiful, lovely, tasty food.

Jacob Batten
Park Junior School, Wellingborough

Hunger

Hunger is blue like the deep blue sea,
It sounds like thunder rumbling in the sky.

It smells like gone-off garbage,
It tastes like a sour lemon.

It feels like a soft, hairy peach,
It looks like a rainy day falling down on me.

It reminds me of a toffee melting in my mouth.

Shannice Chinnery (8)
Park Junior School, Wellingborough

Laughter

Laughter is light red,
Like an Arsenal football top.
It sounds like a whistling whistle.
It tastes like ice cream chocolate sundae.
It smells like egg and bacon on a Sunday.
It looks like my favourite comedy programme.
It feels like a smooth, soft swimming pool,
It reminds me of scoring my first goal,
At the school football club halfway through
The school football club match.

Bayes Day (8)
Park Junior School, Wellingborough

Hunger

Hunger is yellow like the boiling hot sun,
It tastes like very hot spicy curry,
It sounds like a very loud rumbling belly,
It looks like wobbly jelly,
It feels like mushy apple and blueberry pie,
It smells like the blue salty sea,
It reminds me of the largest Pot Noodle.

Jacob Fowle (9)
Park Junior School, Wellingborough

Fear

Fear is pitch-black like the midnight sky,
It sounds like an insane hound talking to the dead,
It smells like a phoenix burning to ash,
It tastes like purple poison,
It feels like burning coal,
It looks like evil Teletubbies,
It reminds me of nightmares after you eat cheese.

Jacob Franklin (8)
Park Junior School, Wellingborough

Laughter

Laughter is yellow like the bright beautiful sun,
It smells like a red beautiful rose,
It tastes like chocolate ice cream with sprinkles,
It sounds like rain falling down on the flowers,
It looks like a smile on my brother's face,
It feels like people hugging each other,
It reminds me of happy and beautiful things.

Leeza Khatun (9)
Park Junior School, Wellingborough

Hunger

Hunger is red like a hot spicy sun,
It smells like mouldy garbage,
It sounds like hungry rumbling tummies,
It tastes like horrible stinky old nappies,
It feels like wobbly jelly on a plate,
It looks like horrible sloppy sick in the toilet,
It reminds me of dark caves with the
Dead old skeletons inside.

Nicole McLeod (8)
Park Junior School, Wellingborough

Fear

Fear is grey like a dusty, black, terrible, dark and doomed old house,
It smells like hot lava in the death,
It looks like there is horror coming closer and closer to your home,
It sounds like a roar from the tear and a hiss is
Like a lady bee,
It tastes like a monster munching in your yoghurt,
It feels like red anger crushing you,
It reminds me of a red devil destroying us all.

Kyle Patel (8)
Park Junior School, Wellingborough

Love

Love is red like red roses,
It feels like a soft, feathery duvet,
It tastes like strawberries,
It smells like candyfloss floating in the sky,
It looks like hot cocoa,
It sounds like a brass band playing,
It reminds me of my friends and family.

Bethany Reid (8)
Park Junior School, Wellingborough

Laughter

Laughter is baby-blue like a midsummer afternoon,
It tastes like a chocolate bar with a marshmallow
In the middle with icing on the top,
It smells like red wine at a wedding in Paris,
It sounds like a million kisses of love,
It looks like a love heart cushion just made,
It feels like a feather that is weightless,
It reminds me of happiness of a lifetime.

Maria Ross (8)
Park Junior School, Wellingborough

Love

Love is red like red roses,
It sounds like my baby screaming,
It tastes like wobbly red jelly,
It smells like my mum's favourite perfume,
It feels like my cuddly teddy growing,
It reminds me of my mum.

Alex Wills (8)
Park Junior School, Wellingborough

Untitled

Laughter is red like the sunrise,
What does it sound like?
It sounds like the swaying wind,
What does it taste like?
It tastes like a double-whipped strawberry ice cream,
With a cherry topping,
With extra strawberry sauce,
What does it smell like?
It smells like the smelly air above you.

Jack Whitworth (8)
Park Junior School, Wellingborough

Hunger

Hunger is red like squishy tomato sauce,
It feels like butterflies in my tummy,
It tastes like a dry bone that has been buried for a million years,
It looks like food that isn't even there,
It sounds like a dinosaur roaring his loudest,
It smells like sausages dipped in tomato sauce,
It reminds me of 100 tonnes of chicken.

Theo Biggs (9)
Park Junior School, Wellingborough

Hunger

Hunger is dark brown,
It smells like a lovely roast dinner,
It tastes like an empty bowl of soup,
It looks like a cup with no juice,
It feels hard and invisible,
It reminds me of a person with no food.

Lucy Miller (8)
Park Junior School, Wellingborough

Hunger

Hunger reminds me a sticky rainbow lollipop,
Hunger smells like fresh air with the sun setting,
Hunger looks like someone fishing in the shimmering shiny ocean,
Hunger tastes like people at a carnival eating choccie candyfloss,
Hunger feels like someone jumping in a swimming
pool that is freezing,
Hunger sounds like a morning sun rising and
Birds singing their songs and
Hunger is pink like the inside of a mouth dripping for tasty food.

Mia Brandon-Smith (8)
Park Junior School, Wellingborough

The Anger Poem

Red is anger, it is like a volcano exploding with hot fire,
It looks like someone is really hot,
It tastes like red soup,
It sounds like someone is very loud,
It reminds me of someone angry,
It smells like someone is sweating,
It feels like someone is going to explode.

Ravine Brownbill (8)
Park Junior School, Wellingborough

Love

Love is pink like Bazooka gum,
It sounds like the ocean,
It tastes like a heart beating,
It smells like chocolate bonbons,
It feels like swimming,
It reminds me of my family.

Savannah Elliott (8)
Park Junior School, Wellingborough

Laughter

Laughter is pink like a big ball bouncing,
It looks like a pink bright flower,
It sounds like the sound of an angel,
It tastes like the way it was not before,
It smells like perfume of a flower growing,
It reminds me of a beautiful sunrise.

Bethany Ellul (9)
Park Junior School, Wellingborough

Anger

Anger is black like the opposite of Heaven,
Getting closer and closer to your heart,
What does anger sound like?
Anger sounds like storm clouds chattering
With a crack of lightning and a gust of howling wind,
What does anger look like?
Anger looks like the terrifying sight of an
Avalanche landing on a crow,
What does anger feel like?
Anger feels like a metal bed with no bed linen or mattress,
What does anger taste like?
Anger tastes like a red-hot chilli pepper burning your mouth,
What does anger smell like?
Anger smells like fresh cow pat moist on a field,
What does anger remind me of?
Anger reminds me of darkness,
Where there is no light.

Claudia Haworth (8)
Park Junior School, Wellingborough

My Laughter Poem

Laughter is yellow like the sand on the beach,
It sounds like the gulls singing in the sky,
It tastes like nice fresh cheese in the fridge,
It smells like a lemon in a pie in the oven,
It feels like the palms of my hands when they go yellow,
It reminds me of my friends when they're nice.

Rowan Lynch (8)
Park Junior School, Wellingborough

Laughter

Laughter is red like the colour of roses,
It sounds like Father Christmas giggling his head off,
It tastes like the sweetest and most delicious sweet ever,
It smells like fish and chips from the fish and chip shop,
It feels like lightning just missing you by luck,
It reminds me of your cheeky smile just like mine.

Muctarr Mansaray (9)
Park Junior School, Wellingborough

Fear

Fear is red like thunder that is loud,
It sounds like cars crashing one after the other,
It tastes like fire in your mouth,
It smells like smoke from a dirty cigarette,
It looks like orange hair sitting in a hairdresser's shop,
It feels like hot spicy peppers drying in the sun,
It reminds me of discrimination.

Aaisha Patel (9)
Park Junior School, Wellingborough

Fear

Fear, what colour is it?
Fear is grey like sadness,
What does it sound like?
It sounds like the groans from an injured soldier,
What does it taste like?
It tastes like mouldy tomatoes,
What does it feel like?
Fear feels like a cut that is mocking you!
What does it look like?
It looks like blood as red as can be,
What does it smell like?
It smells like water washing your hopes away,
What does it remind me of?
It reminds me of being trapped forever.

Kelsey Regan (8)
Park Junior School, Wellingborough

Anger

Red is angry like a volcano erupting with red-hot fire coming down,
It tastes like red-hot chilli pepper in your mouth burning,
It sounds like someone screaming very loudly in the distance,
It looks like sparkling fireworks in the sky
And they are making pictures,
It smells like a burning fire and smoke drifting in the air,
It feels like a crocodile's skin,
It reminds me of a man running down the road,
Very angry indeed!

Jacquieline Sadler (9)
Park Junior School, Wellingborough

Fear

Fear is the colour of scrambled egg mixed with brown paint,
It sounds like a person in a rage getting hit by paint,
It tastes like a feather bathed in a mud bath,
It smells like rotten egg mixed with queen's feet,
It feels like toenails mixed with fish scales,
It looks like a dead bird with ashes all over it,
It reminds me of the Queen in a mudbath!

Ellis Spencer (9)
Park Junior School, Wellingborough

Hunger

Hunger is yellow like something evil with stripes,
It sounds like dinosaurs stamping, looking for dinner,
It looks like round glittery marbles,
It tastes sweet and sour, juicy as well,
It feels lumpy and swishy,
It reminds me of Romans fighting.

Kattie Stoneman (8)
Park Junior School, Wellingborough

Darkness

Lurking in the mists,
Of the deep blue sea,
Or in the haunted playground,
Anywhere he can be.

Drifting down the alleyway,
Underneath the stairs,
Turning crows into ravens
And caves into lairs.

Craig Earl (11)
Park Junior School, Wellingborough

Darkness

Darkness is all around us,
Darkness is everywhere,
In dungeons, cages and graves,
Darkness flies around the world,
Protecting his dark plans,
So be careful where you look,
Darkness might be there.

Kayleigh Torrie (10)
Park Junior School, Wellingborough

What Am I?

Nobody can see me,
I could see rotten children,
The world has been so mean to me,
Nobody can stop me now,
I am going to get them back,
I still have far to go but
I am never going to give up.
What am I?

Revenge.

Jaimini Patel (10)
Park Junior School, Wellingborough

Sadness

Sadness reminds me of when my dog died,
Sadness tastes like rotten cheese,
Stuffed in a sweaty sock,
Sadness feels like rats eating my shoe away,
Sadness looks like a dark black alleyway.

Rhys Sawyer (10)
Park Junior School, Wellingborough

Sweet Love

Roses are red,
Violets are blue,
Love is a disease,
Could I catch it from you?

Sweet as some candy,
As cool as ice,
Everybody knows that,
Love is very nice!

Chocolate is brown,
You can buy it down town
Did you know pink
Makes the boys wink?

Louise Saunders (11)
Park Junior School, Wellingborough

Love

Love is pink, it's Cupid's gift
And he seals it in your heart,
When you meet someone special,
It flies out like a dart,
There's just enough to go around,
It spreads like wildfire,
So next time you feel a slight prick,
Just be careful who you look at,
It might be Cupid's arrow.

Chloe Gidney (10)
Park Junior School, Wellingborough

Fear

Is fear the taste of gum?
I wonder why fear smells like a dead body?
Why does it sound like an owl hooting in the midnight sky?
I wonder why fear is so dark, it is black?
Ouch! It feels so rough around me,
I wonder why it looks like a moonlit street?
Do you know?

Tonika Bing (9)
Park Junior School, Wellingborough

Fear

What does it smell like?
Fear smells like onions,
What colour is it?
Fear is black like the colour of darkness,
What does it look like?
Fear looks like rotten eggs and gone-off custard,
What does it sound like?
Fear sounds like the tap, tap of a tap dripping,
What does it feel like?
Fear feels like a chill running down your spine,
What does it taste like?
Fear tastes like sour lemons,
What does it remind me of?
Fear reminds me being lost and
Not knowing where to go.

Alex Hinds (10)
Park Junior School, Wellingborough

Fear

What does it taste like?
It tastes like mushy peas and custard.

What does it feel like?
It feels like I'm sitting alone in the dark.

What does it smell like?
It smells rotten!

What is the colour of fear?
The colour is black, brown and dull!

Aniqa Hoque (10)
Park Junior School, Wellingborough

Love

It tastes like strawberry jelly,
It smells like a bright red rose,
It looks like a red heart,
It sounds like birds singing in the trees,
It's the colour of red and pink,
It feels really smooth,
It reminds me of Nanny,
What is it?
It's *love!*

Shannon Sanders (9)
Park Junior School, Wellingborough

Laughter

Laughter is funny,
Like runny honey
And hops around like a fluffy bunny.

Laughter makes me happy like
Eating a chocolate bar and saying 'Ha, ha',
Laughter makes me hyper and act like a viper.

Laughter is like the sound of a Hoover,
But not much of a mover,
Laughter is a squiggle
And makes you want to giggle.

Shanile Smith (9)
Park Junior School, Wellingborough

Laughter

Laughter till I die,
Laughter is funny,
Like a hopping bunny,
Wearing a crown,
Also dancing upside down,
It smells like fresh food,
It reminds me of singing to the team,
Rushden and Diamonds,
Cheering them to win,
Ha! Ha! Ha! Ha!

Chloe Stringer (10)
Park Junior School, Wellingborough

Fear

Fear looks like fear and porridge mixed together,
Fear is like spook dust going up your nostrils,
It smells like out-of-date food with rotten apples,
It sounds like doors cracking with ghosts,
It tastes like gas and custard mixed together,
It feels spooky with gross dust.

Dillon Vaghela (9)
Park Junior School, Wellingborough

When I Go Swimming

Swimming is my favourite thing,
I love to go round in the rubber ring,
It's nice to get wet,
So get ready, get set.

We always go on Thursdays after school,
I can't wait to get there and jump in the pool,
I'm learning a tricky stroke, there are quite a few,
It's great to be a swimmer and learn something new.

Graciela Niembro (8)
St Alban's Catholic Primary School, Cambridge

The Seaside

When the seaside is calm,
All the sand lies still,
It's cold, wet, damp while
It rests on the cool ground.

The blue sea makes waves,
That are dangerous which
Make people on boats and
Rescue teams satisfied.

In the long night,
The moon makes a bright light,
Which makes the water,
Calm and shiny.

When it's morning,
The sun rises and
Sparkles round the
World, till birds cheep.

Maurizio Bocchetti (8)
St Alban's Catholic Primary School, Cambridge

The Night

The stars and the moon twinkle like diamonds,
The water sparkles like gems,
The sky is like velvet,
The ground is like rock
And there is where it ends.

Caitlin Wallwork (9)
St Alban's Catholic Primary School, Cambridge

The Spooky Poem

At the dead of night when you're tucked away in bed,
In your darkened garden lies the spooky shed,
The trees rustle all around,
While the grass is spinning round and round.

Spooky at the dead of night,
I will give you quite a fright!
Ghosts creep out from behind trees,
They scare away all the bees.

The scary vampire is always flying around
And zombies are coming out of the ground,
Now here come the big fat ghosts,
They always say they have never ever done a boast.

Christian Wood (8)
St Alban's Catholic Primary School, Cambridge

The Sunset

The sun is calm,
The sun is resting on the beach,
The sun is snoring the wind.

The sun is rising from the beach,
Beautiful as a gem,
But it's as blinding as God.

The sun is whole,
Gentle as a bluebird,
Nice as a smile.

Alexander Carolan (9)
St Alban's Catholic Primary School, Cambridge

A Scary Poem

Be wary of the disgusting troll,
That quietly lies in wait,
To drag you to his smelly hole
And put you on his stinky plate.

His blood is inky and bubbling hot,
He loudly horribly groans,
He'll burn you in his dinner pot,
Your skin, your flesh, your bones.

He'll grind your arms and grab
Your legs and squash you to a pulp,
Then swallow you like a big fat blob,
Munch! Munch! Gulp!

So watch your step when you next go
Upon a silent stroll,
Or you might end in the den below,
As dinner for the troll.

Charlotte Axisa (8)
St Alban's Catholic Primary School, Cambridge

The Invisible Beast

He lives in Transylvannia,
He is the monster of death,
He plays invisible Lacrosse,
He has terrible breath,
He hides, hides and hides,
He gets out his knife,
They immediately fall down,
Almost everyone loses their life.

His feet are like a drum,
He is massive like a gorilla,
He is very strong and bold,
He used to play for Aston Villa,
He was a terrible goalie with 1 cap,
He often had blisters on his hand,
Missiles were chucked at him,
The cheerleaders screamed with the band.

Emmet Lenoach (9)
St Alban's Catholic Primary School, Cambridge

When I Went Into The Trees I Found A Nest Of Bees

When I went into the trees,
I found a nest of bees,
I heard loud growls,
I heard loud howls,
I found a lake
And found a giant snake,
I saw a hound,
I knew it had to be found,
I was in fear,
Then I saw a deer,
The deer was dead
And now the hound has been fed,
I found an ants' nest
And I wanted to take a rest,
But it was 1 o'clock
And I wanted to see a flock,
I saw a load of sheep,
Then it went beep, beep,
When I went into the trees,
I found a nest of bees.

Alfonso Rosse (11)
St Alban's Catholic Primary School, Cambridge

Madame Butterfly

She flitters and flutters in the sky,
A complicated dance manufactured in ancient times,
Her life depends on agility to enable her to fly,
She feels that if she ever stops dancing,
She will be charged for many crimes.

Her wings are of the most perfect symmetry,
She glides gracefully in the breeze,
Her flight is mesmerising and full of ecstasy,
The skill of her travel is performed with the ultimate ease.

She decides to have some recreation time,
Therefore she chooses to rest on a blossom,
This is her favourite way to dine -
Nesting on a blossom eating the sweet flower's pollen.

She flitters and flutters in the sky,
A complicated dance manufactured in ancient times,
She sees with an antenna instead of an eye,
For she is Madame Butterfly.

Natasha Burton (10)
St Alban's Catholic Primary School, Cambridge

Monkeys

Monkeys swinging from tree to tree,
Eating all the bananas,
All they want is to be free,
Otherwise they'll eat your pyjamas.

So when we let them free,
They jump all about,
Having fun and
Being cheeky.

Eve Williams (9)
St Alban's Catholic Primary School, Cambridge

The Invisible Beast

When you're ever at the seaside,
At the dead of night
And suddenly start to feel
An evil awful fright,
There is an invisible beast,
Somewhere on the beach
And you know it's out there somewhere,
When you hear its awful screech.

So when you get into bed that night,
You smell a horrid smell
And you start to wish you were in
A locked up prison cell
And although you cannot see it,
You can feel its hairy hands
And you know you'll never sleep again,
For next to your bed it stands.

Patrick Collins (8)
St Alban's Catholic Primary School, Cambridge

Flashing By

I heard a sound in the distance,
Wondering what I heard,
Then suddenly he grabbed me,
No one heard a word.

In just a sec he left,
I managed to see him go,
Anxiously and nervously I just wanted
To go home.

Then that night I lay in bed,
Terrified and scared,
Then just thought no one would come,
For me in my bed.

Anna McNally (8)
St Alban's Catholic Primary School, Cambridge

The Spiderweb

The spiderweb glistened in the morning sun,
It must be great fun to draw, I'm sure!
Unfortunately the spider that made this one,
Is squashed on the kitchen floor.

Anna Celentano (9)
St Alban's Catholic Primary School, Cambridge

Carnivals

The buzz of excitement is in the air,
Cheering! Shouting! Laughing! Chatting!
Everyone dances around without a care,
The funny costumes shimmer and shine,
They're pink, yellow, blue,
Every colour of the rainbow!
People parade around in a line.

I love the carnival, it's so much fun,
There's popcorn, sweets, choc and candyfloss,
Honeycomb, toffee, candy apples and buns,
If you don't attend the carnival,
Then that's your *loss!*

Eve Stanislawski (11)
St Alban's Catholic Primary School, Cambridge

Silence

Everything is quiet,
As silent as a mouse,
Not even the pitter-patter on the ground,
No talking,
No whispering,
Just the sound of silence,
Until
The ghosts come out to play,
They crash everything over,
They write on walls
And turn all the lights on,
Then everything goes silent again,
But you can still hear
Little elves cleaning the mess.

Samantha Calvey (11)
St Alban's Catholic Primary School, Cambridge

Chocolate

It melts and oozes everywhere,
Dark, milk or white,
Its single taste fills the world,
It's gone with just a bite.

Caramel, coconut and mint,
Orange, nut and coffee,
Honeycomb and Fair Trade,
Rum, brandy and toffee.

Decay, fillings
And missing teeth,
Diabetes and calories,
Heart attack from beneath.

Sarah Taylor (11)
St Alban's Catholic Primary School, Cambridge

Sir McDonald

Sir McDonald is a knight,
Who won't give up on a fight,
He'd fought several dragons
And beaten battalions,
Killed big fat giants
And quietened riots,
He'd beaten bad guys,
But still prefers KFC.

Max Crowther (10)
St Alban's Catholic Primary School, Cambridge

A Poem About Poems

T he poem I am writing
H as
E verything about poems

P oems can be large
O r small
E ven
M assive!

I ngenious

A nd
M arvellous

W eird and
R ealistic
I maginative
T o the letter
I 've not got
N othing but it's there and it's
G one

H ere is happiness
A nd
S adness.

E verything
V ery nearly
E verything
R eally, nearly everything
Y ou won't believe
T hat
H ere
I n this poem
N othing
G oes nowhere, but there's no more space, not fair!

David Joseph Ward (11)
St Alban's Catholic Primary School, Cambridge

The Beauty Of Lorren

This beautiful girl,
This glamorous angel,
The beauty that shows us the light,
Of the world.

She's doing good things,
At everything,
Her mother isn't like her,
Not in one way or another.

Girls are mad,
Girls get sad,
But this one, no, no,
This girl is stunning, smashing and things,
I can't even explain,
How ravishing is she.

We'll call her the angel even though she's Lorren,
Can't think of things better,
That's why we'll call her,
The angel.

Blonde hair has she got,
Brown eyes she has,
Her skin tropical,
Like the Caribbean,
Since this has been said,
Her name is now
The Beauty of Lorren.

Maria-Camila Ferraro (10)
St Alban's Catholic Primary School, Cambridge

Love Is Like Murder

Love, love, lovely love,
Is slobbering slaves' stories,
Or men ruthlessly slaughtered
And freedom desperately sought.

It's always a woman with a dagger and sword
And a man getting extremely bored,
But the men don't know what they're in for
And it's not just a big bore.

They're in for a big fright,
Something they won't believe with human sight,
It's like being killed when you're sleeping
And also when you're not peeping.

And you're in for a big scare,
Something that will make onlookers stare,
Like standing in the Arctic completely bare
And no one really has a care.

You'll never believe,
Love is like murder,
Pulling you in
And teasing you for something you're not going to get.

Oh, it's bloody love,
Murderous love,
Bloodthirsty love,
Murderous love.

Jamie Campbell (11)
St Alban's Catholic Primary School, Cambridge

Seasons

Buds growing, new life coming, lambs spring around the field
Daffodils swaying, snowdrops nodding, blossom
sprinkling the air with fragrance.
Birds sing in the branches, calling out to the spring.
The sun peeps out from behind the clouds
And swallows up the darkness.

Bees buzz from bloom to bloom
Butterflies dance in the air
Cool ice cream melts in mouths
White waves rush the sandy beach
Sun sparkles on the water.

Leaves falling, turning brown, red and yellow
Join the ones below with a gentle rustle.
Wind picks them up, whirling them round in his mighty hand.
Mothers and fathers come out to rake the ground
Children race to kick the growing piles.

The birds have flown south, the snow comes,
Soft, freezing drifts
Children hurtle downhill on their toboggans,
Colliding with heaps of white.
Families swing downstairs to find presents under the tree.

Alexander Tudor (11)
St Aubyn's Preparatory School, Woodford Green

Someone I Know

I see someone I know
Who might pass away
She cries when I cry
Because cancer is on the way.

She is so strong and bold
I know she will live
But my heart truly aches
That it will, for I cannot give.

She is never wrong
And always so right
She never goes
Without a willing fight.

My mum, I shall thank
For getting me through
We share the same pain
Of too much of loving you.

Emily Balcombe (11)
St Aubyn's Preparatory School, Woodford Green

The Polar Bear

The great white bear perched on the edge of the ice,
As he lapped up the water - it tasted quite nice.

The ice beneath him suddenly broke away,
So from the sea he watched what happened that day.

The kingdom of ice where he once had fun
Began melting away, under the sun.

He froze, wanting to swim,
But the water around him looked scary and dim.

If he swam, where would he go?
Beneath the waves' rapid flow.

The land he had loved came in tumbling heaps,
And crashed into the seas' evil deeps.

The bear had known his kingdom would fall,
But he never expected it to plunge into the world's biggest pool.

Isabel Roberts (11)
St Aubyn's Preparatory School, Woodford Green

Wind

Wild wind whipping the damp green grass,
Strong as a bristling bull.
Crowds of people running into their homes saying,
'It is very powerful!'

Wind whistling through the holes in the houses,
Like a secret, silent singer.
A small child sucking the biting frostbites,
On his tiny frozen finger.

Nobody can go anywhere outside,
The wind acting like a terrible tyrant.
The terrified families letting anyone come inside,
Only hearing the crying infants.

Whirling wind swirling over the treetops,
On the wall it has the petrified people pinned.
Now the city is left in destruction,
All because of the wind.

Raoul Akhtar (10)
St Aubyn's Preparatory School, Woodford Green

Winter

Blistering blowing blizzards tear through the air,
It's enough to give anyone a scare!
Freezing frost floats gently down,
Gradually, quietly, creating no sound.

Cheery children caper in the snow,
While abundant adults stay as extinct as dodos.
Snowmen appear here and there,
Created by a child's great care.

Christmas is a joy to everyone,
Whether religious, or just to have fun!
Then comes terrific New Year's Day,
And no one can keep the fiery fireworks at bay!

Winter, like everything, has its ups and its downs,
The snow, the fun, and the great snow mounds.
And finally comes chilly weather which brings dull moods
And, alas, the winter description concludes.

Sandeep Vijayakumar (10)
St Aubyn's Preparatory School, Woodford Green

The Superb Snow

Snow creeps upon you like a white ghost
Falling from the deep white sky
Nobody knows where it comes from
Turning roofs from brown to white
It's as crunchy as cornflakes
But when you touch it
It's soft velvet.
Finally the golden coin up in the sky comes out
And the snow dies away
Melting like an ice cream.
The grass is back to green
And the ponds are back to flowing water
But the snow will be back soon.

Saira Rafiq (11)
St Aubyn's Preparatory School, Woodford Green

Warming

Painless to think
We're melting the world away
This talk of global warming
Filling our ears these days.

Worried about temperature
Like everyone else
Do something about it
This is not a trend.

Global warming is important
More than you could ever believe
I think it's not too late to turn off
That light you left on in your house.

The signs were twenty years ago
The action is now
It's not too late
To make your statement now.

Olufemi Femi-Gureje (11)
St Aubyn's Preparatory School, Woodford Green

Thunder

Its colour is pitch-black like an ugly witch's dress.
It feels like a thousand pins falling onto your delicate neck
and gives shivers down your spine.
Thunder looks like a charging rhino,
ready to have you eaten for its tea.
It tastes like bitter salad without dressing or flavouring.
Thunder sounds like an angry god
that has seen someone worshipping another model
and not himself and him.
It smells of rotten eggs, stuffed with out-of-date blue Stilton,
smeared over with sour milk with skin on top.
Thunder reminds you of a recent accident,
a picture that frightened you in the dead of night.

Pierre Fleet (11)
St Aubyn's Preparatory School, Woodford Green

Next Year Mr Sloth

In moving slow he has no peer.
You ask him something in the ear.
He thinks about it for a year.

He gives you an answer next year.
And you wonder why it took a year.
You wonder why so simple and clear.

He wakes up with a deer.
A deer sore and wet.
Bleeding from a net.

A net tight around him.
Bleeding badly, super sore.
The sloth helps him with care.

The deer recovers next year.
In return the deer takes him to a fair.

Then off to sleep he goes.
Still swaying gently from his toes
And you know he knows, he knows.

Theo Simpson
St Aubyn's Preparatory School, Woodford Green

The Devil

The Devil looks like fear in one's eye
With the gift to sniff out anything,
Its eyes are no more than slits in its skin
With death stuck inside every sin.

Its horns are snipping scissors shredding strangers swiftly
Their decayed teeth are daggers dangerously digging death into skin
A waft of this creepy creature's breath will kill off the strongest men
This weird beast has the most muscular physique,
Which will make the strongest man look like a timid mouse.

This unidentified animal has no legs as all
Its feet are in fact colossal, going *crash, bang, wallop!*
As they thud against the lava-filled floor
Unlike the Devil
Everyone's feet are like cats' on a hot tin roof
When they touch the ground which is made of heated liquid.

To me these are the most terrible monsters known to Man
Then again can you think of a more deadly beast?

Bethany Lamb (11)
St Aubyn's Preparatory School, Woodford Green

Thierry Henry

T he best player in the football world
H igh profile footballer scoring goals as fast as a bullet
I am the number one fan of him
E very match I go to
R unning faster than a cheetah
R ubbish, ridiculous referees
Y ou should admire him

H ero of Arsenal FC
E very match he scores a goal
N ot one match does he go without scoring
R oaring crowds screaming his name
Y oung children as Arsenal mascots.

Danny Twomey (10)
St Aubyn's Preparatory School, Woodford Green

Snowflakes

S wirling, twirling, falling down softly
N o more sun but snow is in the air
O nly staying till the sun comes out again
W hen snow comes out everybody is smiling
F rom the time that snowflakes tumble,
there is happiness in the air
L ayers and layers of snow coming through
A lovely thick layer of pure white snow
K ind children helping elderly people
E verybody is playing in the snow happily
S nowmen of all shapes standing proud.

Bianca Muswell (10)
St Aubyn's Preparatory School, Woodford Green

Fireworks Are Fabulous

Fireworks are elaborate
An illusion to all,
Stimulating anyone who dares unleash these screaming monsters
They screech and squirm
As they emerge from the darkness of the midnight sky!

When they hit the tip of the world,
An eruption begins, like a volcano
Spurting its lava everywhere and anywhere
Colours whizz up to the sky, shattering into a million tiny pieces
Bronze, aqua and crimson, luminating the world below them!

Fireworks are a beautiful sight
For one's eyes to see.
Thousands upon thousands of twinkling stars,
Rain down on you.
Fireworks are fabulous!

Sarah Parker (11)
St Aubyn's Preparatory School, Woodford Green

My Ferret Tommy

F luffy, furry, fancy, fantastic, friendly, fragile ferrets.
E yes can tell when they are scared, as their endless tail
spikes up like a porcupine and lets off a terrible smell.
R osy red gums and rotten teeth, should be scrubbed
at least twice a week.
R apidly running round and round, playing with toys
and enjoying itself as much as it can.
E xciting, endless times you can have,
especially with the ferret I had.
T ommy was his name and he always used to play silly games,
as well as trying to escape.
S oft and silky was his fur, how I miss my ferret Tommy.

Helena Ruffy (11)
St Aubyn's Preparatory School, Woodford Green

Pride

Pride is crimson with a hint of dark blue.
It reminds me of a subtle student just graduated from university.
It feels like a person gritting their hard, sharp teeth.
It tastes like sizzling sausages sizzling in a scorching skillet.
It looks like a burning fire, scrunching up heated newspaper.
It smells like hot rain dripping down from the dark sky.

Michael Palser (10)
St Aubyn's Preparatory School, Woodford Green

Lost In The World

Hiding behind the towering rock
Thinking to myself
I am not scared, how could I be?
Trying not to tremble in fear
I pounce proudly from my hideout
Impressing the visitors
As I do my opening act.

On the other side of the metal bars
A man passes by.
He studies me, fascinatingly
As though he has never seen my type before
I am irritated by the way he looks at me
With his beady eyes
Feeling devastated, whilst trying to hide my tears
I roar an *enormous* roar
Enough to shake the sturdiest building
But not enough to frighten him away.

Though I used to wonder
What happened to the brave beast?
The wise leader who was wild at heart?
As time passed on, I realised
That the cold-hearted humans
Taught me to hate
Taught me to kill
I feel as though I'm a raging fire, inside,
Destroying everything.

But Hell is beside me
Trying to trap me
A cowardly prisoner outside
But on the inside, I know who I am
A majestic lion, lost in the world.

Azura Wicaksono (10)
St Aubyn's Preparatory School, Woodford Green

Wonder

W onder is a tall twinkling throne lifting you to cloud nine
O pening up a new door inside your brain.
N ewly opened presents in thought creeps into mind.
D azzling white is the colour
E very day it must occur though not at good times maybe.
R ain or shine you can't escape it.

W orking hard throughout the day leads you to wonder
O verall it's like clouds
N ever-ending strings
D reamy waves inside yourself like the ones in the sea
E ven the smartest people do
R eally quite hard to get over.

W onder is the sweet smell of candyfloss
O ozing with sugary flavour
N ice squishy cushion is the touch
D aytime dreams occur
E xtremely inquisitive
R eady to wonder at any time.

Rosie Henderson (11)
St Aubyn's Preparatory School, Woodford Green

Snowing

S now is falling from the night sky, fresh and white,
drifting to the ground
N othing is better than a white blanket of snow in the moonlight.
O nly if there was snow every single day, when you wake up
in the morning.
W ow! Look at all this snow we say as we wake up
to see a winter wonderland!
I cicles hanging from the houses, glinting in the light
like diamonds.
N ow the snow is melting and our fun is as if it is drifting away.
G one after a day the snow is turning into horrible mushy slush.

Ryan Euesden (10)
St Aubyn's Preparatory School, Woodford Green

Seasons

S ummer is hot, like a raging fire
U nder a shadow, burning in a heap
M ums and dads kissing romantically in the pool
M ums putting slimy cream on your skin
E ars have caught alight in a ferocious fire
R apid fireballs shooting at me.

W eather is very cold, frozen ponds cracking
I ntersport selling hot fiery gloves
N aughty children throwing snowballs at cars
T eam red is beating the blues at the snowball fight
E veryone is ice skating with the ducks
R ound balls of snow falling.

Dominic Fox (10)
St Aubyn's Preparatory School, Woodford Green

Anger

Anger is the sound of the roaring sun being annihilated.
Anger can taste like sour sweets paralysing my tongue.
Anger smells of bad perfume burning your skin.
Anger shows the rage in someone's eyes from their heart.
Anger drains out your feelings one by one.
Anger is the feeling that stops you from succeeding.

Raheel Akhtar (11)
St Aubyn's Preparatory School, Woodford Green

Anger

Anger is like a volcano erupting with lava.
Anger is the taste of bitter herbs going into your mouth.
Anger looks like a fire burning down a house.
Anger is when I lose a football match.
Anger sounds like someone's car breaking down.
Anger smells like old cheese that has gone off.
Anger feels like touching a spiky hedgehog.

Peter Kilpatrick (11)
St Aubyn's Preparatory School, Woodford Green

A Recipe For Anger

One hot bowl of tomato soup
One hot chilli pepper
A few spicy herbs
A dash of curry powder

Mix together over a hot flame
Add a sprinkle of black pepper
A teaspoon of tabasco
And a dollop of English mustard

Wait for the heat to rise
From the tips of your toes
To the hairs on your head
Now watch the heat erupt.

William Bryan (10)
St Aubyn's Preparatory School, Woodford Green

Thunderstorm

The lightning slashed at the murky sky,
The sound itself can make a plant die,
The wind howled and screamed at the waves,
Striking the boat; killing slaves,
The booming thunder shook the sky
Which of course made the wind cry,
It screamed with the highest voice,
The captain said, 'I have no choice,
Give the call to abandon ship!'
We could see his juddering lip,
The skies crackled through the clouds,
The people screaming, yes screaming crowds,
The lightning struck, the boat on fire,
We saw the helicopter, what a flier.

That was the end of my little tale
But it is to be remembered when you set sail.

Alex Goodier (10)
St Aubyn's Preparatory School, Woodford Green

Winter

The claws of a cat pulling the wind towards me,
Whilst the wind hailing like an owl trying to find a friend,
Instead of producing rain why can't it make me a hot cup of tea?
It needs to fix my window as glass is scattered everywhere.

The rain forming a swimming pool as deep as a well,
People having to change their clothes every hour,
Everyone shouting, frostbite feels like Hell,
And people getting the taste of bitter herbs.

The snow was a white blanket dazzling like a diamond ring,
It felt like the world had turned into ice as cold as the tap
could possibly go,
With snowmen looking as bored as the only whale in the ocean,
well so did everyone,
And mums having to go out to get more carrots
especially as Christmas is coming up!

Grace Emanuel (11)
St Aubyn's Preparatory School, Woodford Green

Autumn

Autumn is the fourth season,
that's cold, grey and gloomy.
It gathers out the silent wind
to blow away the leaves.
It starts to make the rain fall
and grow food for the winter.

Autumn is a time for coats
to be worn with pride.
It's a time where illness starts
and spring is where it ends.
Autumn reminds me of a freezing day
where the climate is under average.

Montaz Marché (10)
St Aubyn's Preparatory School, Woodford Green

Dillie

Dillie is as sneaky as a fox,
I call her Silly Dilly,
A black and white springer spaniel,
Always up to mischief.

She is very hyper,
Mainly around me,
She's nervous of other dogs she meets,
But she's become much braver.

When Dillie misbehaves,
Like when she goes upstairs,
Usually she gets told off,
But she just wags her tail.

When Dillie has her training,
It's up to her to work,
But she'll only work if she's in the mood,
And usually she's not.

Dillie's very friendly though,
She loves to mess around,
She has a brilliant temperament,
But really she's a clown.

Mirran Trimble (10)
St Aubyn's Preparatory School, Woodford Green

Summer Versus Winter

S hooting bullets from the silvery skies,
N ow the whole world is being ruled by this white king
O ver the world he unfolds his army,
W hat is the reason for this great war?

The empire is crumbling
Mother Nature now has a new face,
Light rays from the sun break through the barrier,
The white king watches as his army is defeated,
But he knows he will administer the sky once again.

S ummer now rules all,
U nited as one they destroy the winter and the silvery skies,
N othing can stop Summer's greatest weapon . . . not even itself.

David Abe (10)
St Aubyn's Preparatory School, Woodford Green

Happiness

Happiness is glowing white
Like snowdrops falling from Heaven.

It sounds like a voice from God
It tastes like the coldest chill from Norway!

It smells like a fresh perfume,
It looks like Heaven is falling,
It feels like a gleaming monster.

Tom Boyd (11)
St Aubyn's Preparatory School, Woodford Green

Friends

I once had a loyal friend,
she was like my only sister.
We stuck together when times were bad,
we were best buddies until now.

We parted our ways
on a grey gloomy day.
My heart sank like a stone plunged into water.

Every day I walked alone
with a cloud above my head, striking me with lightning of sadness.
It was like my heart was gone,
it was like my happiness was banished.

I walked around with my head dropped low,
like a chain hanging from a person's neck.
My heart was not red, not pink,
but gloomy grey and black.

Every day waking up to the sun.
Every day doing a chore of going to school.
It was horrible without her.
She was the spark of my life.

And now the spark has faded, faded away.
I am over it now, that was a long time ago.
But I really am over it,
I am alone.

Jasmine Brown-Rasé
St Aubyn's Preparatory School, Woodford Green

The Dark Shadow

He is older than me
He is taller than me
He's nasty
His words are mean.

His actions hurt
His anger is unfair
He's powerful.

He's in the school
He's on the playground
He's on the bus
He gives mean stares.

He scares me.
He's like a dark shadow.

Jai Singh Bance
St Aubyn's Preparatory School, Woodford Green

My Idol

M y idol is the most reliable person
Y ou can hear him from a mile away

I like him as a mate
D oing the best any can do
O h why can't I be like him?
L ike that person over there
S o I look at him all the time to see how I can improve

His name is Mark.

M is for manners
A is for acceptable
R is for ready
K is for kind.

Harry Puncher (10)
St Aubyn's Preparatory School, Woodford Green

I Hate My Homework

I hate to do
My homework,
It makes me feel
So bad.

Every day
By my desk,
It makes me
Go mad.

When I go
To school,
The teachers have
Had enough.

They rip their
Shirts to the floor,
(What a bad sight).

They go to a room,
Then get taken to a home,
They also like these
Men in white,
Who are taking them away.

(I am used to this).

Charlie Stockings (11)
St Aubyn's Preparatory School, Woodford Green

Favourite Thing

The favourite thing is my pet cat;
good, nice and active like a midnight bat.
Her name is Khushu, swift like an arrow,
and thought is a cat likes climbing trees,
in the manner of how a gorilla frees.

Her eyes are evergreen bright,
tries to observe her big surroundings.
Her nose is as black as the depths of the sea.
Ready to have the smell of food;
and while stealing she is successful.

On the pavement,
she crawls by.
Giving strangers her glimpse of shine.
While she goes on her little run,
she never forgets to give herself fun.

As she returns home, she lets me pat her
then she has her dinner, eating like a big growling bear.
And finally, as tired as a tiny ant,
she cuddles up in her warm comfy bed and soon goes to sleep.

Rucha Kelkar (11)
St Aubyn's Preparatory School, Woodford Green

The Wolf

The wolf is a ghost,
that moves silently through the blanket of white snow,
leaving perfect footprints.
His thick woolly grey coat dances in the cold whistling wind.
His powerful howl echoes through the tall never-ending trees.
He sits up with his body bold and glances at the ghostly
galleon of the moon.
His claws are like hazardous daggers as sharp
as the top of a mountain.
His teeth are sharp and pierce every inch of the animal's body
that it devours.
His nose always sniffing, his eyes seeing all.
He moves swiftly through the snow,
his ears alert, ready for lurking danger known as Man.
Bang!
As the mighty wolf lays, taking his last breath,
a new mighty wolf cub is born.

Shauna O'Malley
St Aubyn's Preparatory School, Woodford Green

The Moon

The big bright moon comes out at night
Shining radiantly, glowing light.

The huge grey wolf howling at it, mad
If you can't see, it's not that bad.

The sun reflects onto the moon
But it will go down very soon.

When you wake up it might be gone
Sometimes it can be very long.

It orbits round and round the Earth
It shines all night for worth

As it travels round the Earth!

Samuel Bromley (11)
St Aubyn's Preparatory School, Woodford Green

Amber In The Snow

The snow is deep,
The snow is cold,
It feels rough on my warm coat.

Then I feel it on my tummy,
As I tremble through the thickness of the snow,
I feel cold and tired.

I get home and lie by the blazing fire,
My owner rubs my belly,
As she listens to Christmas music, I fall asleep.

I dream I am far away, in a warm place
With mountains of bones and rivers of ice-cold water.
I love this place, I never want to go.

Rachel Collin (11)
St Aubyn's Preparatory School, Woodford Green

Cat

She is sleek and beautiful,
She is delicate and elegant,
She is swift and silent,
She is creeping softly,
She is hunting cunningly,
She is tiptoeing through the long grass,
She is approaching her helpless prey,
She is leaping through the air as if she weighs an ounce:
This is the moment in which the cunning cat will pounce.

The cat is like a crawling shadow, creeps back to her den,
To feed her cubs who squirm like worms and are furry balls of fluff;
Then the cat takes them by the scruff and cleans their silky fur.
They scowl and try to wriggle away and miaow and run
and crawl to play.

Jennifer Richards (11)
St Aubyn's Preparatory School, Woodford Green

Harry The Horse

H arry my horse has such smooth, silky skin,
that shines like crystal clear diamonds.
O rganic orange skin is fed and given to him.
R ipe, red, rosy apples is what Harry likes the most,
but he doesn't like to boast.
S leeping horses lay on their chest for a rest,
after their Sunday roast.
E veryone enjoys riding these beautiful, wonderful horses
especially my horse Harry.
S o come and join in the fun with riding horses
on race courses, using Harry's friend Barry.

Omrita Lancaster-Khosla
St Aubyn's Preparatory School, Woodford Green

I Am Winter

I am Winter,
Engulfed in my crisp pallid skin.
My lips are of ice,
My hair is of frost,
My eyes are blinded in loss.
Cold-hearted, I shall bite again.
My cunning mind shall plot.
While the enemy burns his fearsome rays,
I shall sit in peace,
Awaiting the time of revenge.

I am Winter,
In my velvet veil of snow,
Wrapped up, all in white,
While the mist swarms my coat.
I shall relax in harmony, in my tomb of ice,
Enjoying the watchful, comfortable nights.
While the other seasons slave away,
It's time to plan the future days.

I am Winter.
The time has come.
I rejoice with my friends,
Conjuring them up, one by one:
The blizzards, the hail, the storms, the fun.
I am *Winter.*

Minying Huang (10)
St Faith's School, Cambridge

What Am I?

I am here when you don't want me!
I get everywhere possible!
Where people can't have me!
I can't help being loud, it's my nature!
I am sometimes blue and sometimes yellow!
I am here sometimes and not others.
You can't ask for me, you just have to wait.
My mood swings, you can't avoid them, they just happen!
I like metal! I like cars!
Occasionally I like to hurt you!
Don't ever hold a golf club under a tree!

I am lightning.

Hannah Leighfield (11)
St Faith's School, Cambridge

I Am A Rainbow

I am a rainbow.
I appear after a storm.
You can find me in a field or on any piece of land.

In my multicoloured jacket and my blue summer hat
I cover acres of land with my beauty of colours.
I have two eyes and two arms, but no legs.

I don't last forever and you can't touch me.
I am just an image, not a straight figure.

Athena Hart (11)
St Faith's School, Cambridge

The Shadow Man

I stand alone in this dark life,
My dreams so far away,
I ponder how I may prevail,
'Gainst the anger of the coming day.

My heart has withered, cracked and died,
A testament of hurt,
My tears do not fall anymore,
I have no more I've learnt,

More time I spend alone, entombed,
My soul away, away,
My quivering hands begin to shake,
As I start to fall away.

Miranda Davies (11)
St Faith's School, Cambridge

Autumn

I am Autumn

Soft skin, brown-eyed and brave-hearted,
Wrapped in a coat covered with scarlet leaves
And sandals upon my feet I wear,
In a cosy log cabin in a clearing among the trees I live,
When my time comes, I dance among the plants
Making them curl and turn red, yellow and brown,
My friends are the birds and the deer,
They comfort me when I'm lonely,
When Summer has his turn,
I eat the fruits he makes upon my trees
My home is my holiday,
The trees swaying in the wind
Like they're singing happily to me,
Trapped in a dome full of life,
Wherever I go,
I am Autumn.

Alice Kendall (10)
St Faith's School, Cambridge

Spring

I am Spring.

Smooth skin, lousy are my black eyes
but impeccable is my hearing.

Black eyes and brown skin,
forward goes my cylindrical body.

Speed and strength have I,
alongside my chocolate-brown camouflage
to match the chocolate-brown earth.

Under your feet in the turf I lie,
pushing winter out and making a path
for the beloved summer to shine out.

As I brush past the bulbs,
giving them a signal to open up
and give out their wondrous wonders.

Crawling along, munching away
at the throttling weeds, helping my pretty friends.

I am Spring.

Henry Fairey (10)
St Faith's School, Cambridge

Dragons

Mystical beings roamed the land,
They soared across oceans, with riders at hand.
Wings long as houses, scales glisten in the moon,
Who knows? They'll be back soon.

Surreptitious eyes 'round every corner,
Breath full of flames, hotter than a sauna.
Life that is infinite, we entitle them as light,
Someone would be lucky, if they got a flight.

They ruled the Earth, and the magic ruled them,
But then a dark cloud came, an evil gem.
It wanted the power, but could not acquire,
But it kept trying, to be called Sire.

They fought for their race, for magic to live on,
But before we knew it, all had gone.
The gem had won, but not all is lost,
The dragons will rise again, despite the frost.

Abigail Routsis (11)
St Faith's School, Cambridge

Waves

I am the sea
Pale water passing by
Hitting the rocks
Sometimes I am happy and sometimes I am sad
When I am sad, I knock things down
When I am happy, I am just like white horses trotting by.
You can see me, I am shining when I am happy but small
Sometimes I can be large, as big as an elephant
Sometimes I can just fly away from the sea
Into the sky and into the stars.

Ryan Sparkes (10)
St Faith's School, Cambridge

Spring

I am Spring,
Ornate and small,
My heart of love,
My soul of good,
My presence of peace.

A veil of love upon my shoulders,
And lance of righteousness in my hand,
The flowers beautiful and crisp,
Obey my every command.

Bryn Kendrick-Jones (10)
St Faith's School, Cambridge

Impossible Questions

What are caves?
Caves are the eyes of God,
Caves are the shelter of nature,
Caves are the all-seeing eyes,
Caves gave freedom to our ancestors,
Caves gave us things we need.

What are mountains?
Mountains are one of God's creations,
Mountains give eagles a place to stay,
Mountains are snow-glazed points,
Mountains gave us things we need.

What is the universe?
The universe is a light and dark unknown,
The universe gave us Earth,
The universe was made to make us think.

Matthew Holl (11)
St Faith's School, Cambridge

I Am Summer

I am Summer
Smooth English rose skin, soft eyes and a warm heart
Wrapped in my velvet veil of sunburnt red shorts
And a baby-blue shirt
Lying in my cosy solar system
As hot as the sun.

Emily Cox (10)
St Faith's School, Cambridge

The Abominable Snowman

The abominable snowman,
Once gave us a bomb,
We found it under the Christmas tree,
The tag said 'From Tom!'

He stole my blue scarf,
And my dad's fave woolly hat,
He even took fur,
From the tabby cat!

Outside he stood with a face of death,
After eating the carrot he had stinky breath,
Now he stands with the buttons on his belly,
He looks like a stale inedible jelly!

You see his tummy really big,
He looks a bit like a pig,
But there's his face, angry and strong,
You know you're not alive for long!

Phoebe Hyde (10)
St Faith's School, Cambridge

I Am Summer

With my tall burning body, flame-hot hands
I fire upon the world.
Wearing my ash-hot cloak, with my sun-scorched shoes
In my fireball of light and heat
Surrounded by endless deserts.
I bring life and heat throughout the warm summer and spring.
Juggling my fireballs, eating my hot food.

Christian Westrip (10)
St Faith's School, Cambridge

Night

Like a sparkling spider's web
the moon glowed,
raindrops dripped down the windowpane
like melon dribbling down a baby's chin,
like a silk duvet cover,
slithering off the bed
mist slides through the air.

Megan Simmonds (11)
St Faith's School, Cambridge

I Am Summer

Encrusted in a friendly glare,
heart of saffron glow,
fire flicker waded skirt,
silk desert scared my face,
I'm hidden in an ash of life,
unhappiness and despair
breath of chiffon brocade
casting shadow of heat,
I fly and run
from the cold crystal winter
forever thinking about life
on the bubbling sun.

I am Summer.

Lara Webber (11)
St Faith's School, Cambridge

Storm

When midnight arrives so does the storm,
Merciless beams shoot down for attack,
Noises surround cities and streets,
Rain thunders down,
The storm is angry,
Wants its own way.

Sasha York (10)
St Faith's School, Cambridge

The Wild Storm

The peevish water splintered
the rocks' centre causing a great cacophony.
After the cantankerous water,
ricocheted off the resisting rocks,
then it drew in again,
catching a breath for another awesome attack.

James Cassidy (10)
St Faith's School, Cambridge

I Am Winter

Hard as ice, emotions of steel and a heart of white.
Coated in crystals and a pebble white blanket,
boots of silver like sapphire.
I live in the mountains, hot is cold, caves of immortal frost.
I play with hurricanes and toy with death,
the ice cap is my playground.
I dream of the icy temples in the depths of the Arctic winds,
and I bathe in the wrath of the frozen lake.

Lucas Wood (11)
St Faith's School, Cambridge

I Am Summer

I am Summer.
Scorching skin like flames, heart of sun,
coat of sweat, boots of wax,
keeping my candle brain perched.
Living in a dry air of desert, waterless,
making water rise,
rays of sun, my only friend,
keeping me through the evil frost of winter,
ever dreaming of Bahamas' boiling heat.
I am Summer.

Willa Sedgwick Rough (11)
St Faith's School, Cambridge

I Am Summer

I am Summer
Huge eyes, heart of emotion,
Coated by hot titan sun,
I am stranded, inside hot summer sun,
Boxed in a world of heat.

Jessie Sharp (11)
St Faith's School, Cambridge

I Am Looking At You

As I look at you,
Do you feel my sorrow?
Do you feel my hatred?

Can you hear the terror?
Trapped within my mind.
The thought of my life burns away like wood and fire.
Nothing can repent my fear,
Nothing now can heal me.

As I look at you,
Can you feel my sorrow?
Can you feel the tears of memory,
Drifting down my cheek?
My life is slowly ending
Now there's nothing left for me.

Tom Elmslie (11)
St Faith's School, Cambridge

Spring

I am Spring
Gentle-eyed, soft-hearted
Clothed in flowers' silky petals
Young leaves make my shoes
I live in fields of spring flowers
Boxed in soft grasses
I bring sunlight, flowers and happiness
I am Spring.

Kathryn Hawkins (10)
St Faith's School, Cambridge

I Am Summer

As a volcano I erupt,
The waxy fingers melt away,
Emotionless as your veins,
Covered in crimson skin,
Wearing summer sandals,
Curtained in palm tree shirts of zinnober,
Living in my palace of boiling mercury,
Boxed in happiness of the sun,
Sending summer storms of lightning.

Alex Pritchard (10)
St Faith's School, Cambridge

I Am Winter

White skin, sharp-eyed and black-hearted,
Covered in a white leather coat with snow as my hair.
Ice drips down my cheeks.
As summer comes out, I live in the darkest and deepest mountain.
I am Winter!

Fergus England (10)
St Faith's School, Cambridge

Love

Love is like a beautiful white shining dove.
Love sounds like a heart beating real fast.
Love feels like beautiful soft music.
Love smells like a bunch of roses.
Love looks like a humungous sunflower in the sun.
Love reminds me of the time I had a girlfriend.

Dillan Berry (10)
St Joseph's Junior School, Luton

If You Were By The Stream

If you were by the stream
What would you do?
Jump, shout, mess about
Or say that I love you?

If you were by the stream
What would you smell?
Cat, rat, half-eaten hat
Or a cow that's lost its bell?

If you were by the stream
What would you touch?
Spider, mouse, big green house
Or a boy that misses his mum so much?

If you were by the stream
What would you hear?
Mama, Papa, badly working car
Or a girl having her mum clean her ear?

If you were by the stream
What would you see?
Cup, plant, someone saying I can't
Or a big, gorgeous painting of me?

If you were by the stream
What would you taste?
Crisps, grime, snails' slime
Or a bucket of garbage waste?

If you were by the stream
What would you say?
Ah, ohh, I need the loo
Or hip hip hooray?

Munashe Chagonda (9)
St Margaret's CE (VA) Primary School, Ipswich

The Joy Of Christmas Eve

The joy of Christmas Eve,
Yes, the nights I'll never forget,
Check my stocking's in place,
And that everything else is set.

Say goodnight to the pets,
And the same to Mother,
Snuggle into bed,
Pull up the cover.

Feel a shimmer of excitement,
All nice and warm,
Cup your hands together,
Oh, I can't wait till dawn!

And then it's Christmas Day,
With lots of people and gifts,
Nanny and Grandad,
Yes, they're all here
What a wonderful Christmas gift list.

Father Christmas has come,
Oh, all these pressies to keep,
All this wonderful joy,
It makes my heart leap.

I love all the happiness,
That everyone receives,
But I will never forget,
The joy of Christmas Eve!

Victoria Maudsley (10)
St Margaret's CE (VA) Primary School, Ipswich

My Pet

My pet is lazy, my pet drinks milk,
My pet's furry body feels like silk,
My pet is silly, my pet is crazy,
Because my pet is my kitten, Maisy!

Alice Fisher (9)
St Margaret's CE (VA) Primary School, Ipswich

Polar Bear

A fluffy mate
A rolling weight

As white as snow
A friend or foe

As cold as ice
A sacrifice

A fierce hunter
A loud grunter

Will it always be there
To make me polar bear?

Tori Saunders (10)
St Margaret's CE (VA) Primary School, Ipswich

Owl Kennings

A wing flapper,
A day napper,

A big bird,
A clever nerd,

A one so wise,
A pair of eyes,

A tree sleeper,
A nest keeper,

A dinner fowl,
To make me an owl.

Abigail Williamson (10)
St Margaret's CE (VA) Primary School, Ipswich

Quest

The old mighty dragon,
Lives in a dragon's lair,
Tearing down the village,
Eating all the wares.
We all need a hero to slay the mighty one,
Here comes our hero - Sir Peter the Strong!
They fight a mighty battle,
But the winner is the prince,
Now the ruler of the dragon's lair,
Chops off all the dragon's hair!

Michael Collins (7)
St Thomas More's Catholic Primary School, Colchester

If You're Going To The Zoo

If you're going to the zoo . . .

Then be careful you don't chew
For the monkeys will hear
And will make a horrible cheer
They'll also rattle the bars with noise
And trust me, you'd rather chat to the boys!

If you're going to the zoo
Then you should first go to Sue
For she'll give you advice
To first visit the mice
There are about six of them
But your mum wouldn't think they're little gems

If you're going to the zoo
Then visit the old grey kangaroo
For she has three beautiful babies
Always crowded as if they're celebrities
After that you must go to the giraffes
For they will always make you laugh.

If you're going to the zoo
Then please only go once on the canoe
For you need to spend most of your time with the lions instead,
Because they're hardly ever asleep in their bed.
They are all very furry and loud,
And their breath will shoot you to a cloud.

If you're going to the zoo
Then go to the penguins who never flew
And they'll be fed if it's your big day,
Also, if you're good,
You might get mini fireworks on your cake, hey!

Jessie Grimsey (10)
St Thomas More's Catholic Primary School, Colchester

My Rabbit

My rabbit crouches then leaps in the air with its legs in the sky,
Its whiskers are wiggly and twitchy,
It sniffs out food then hides in the garden
Waiting for someone to come,
Then it leaps up in the air like an Olympic jumper
To see if I have food,
Then it goes in its home and sleeps rabbit dreams.

Saskia Cooke (8)
St Thomas More's Catholic Primary School, Colchester

Rain

I turn the sky dark.
I spit at your house.
I throw hailstones at you.
I make floods as big as rivers.
I produce terrifying storms
That are so dangerous they could kill you.
I soak your clothes right through.
I feel calm now my horrible work is over,
Now I will let the sun have its turn.

Elena Richards (9)
St Thomas More's Catholic Primary School, Colchester

The Rain

I help the plants grow for you to eat
I clean up dirt so you don't have to.

I hurt people with my stones of ice.
I blow up electric currents with lightning.
I smash windows just by clapping my hands.
I can electrocute a tree and set it on fire.
I flood small towns and destroy people's houses,
Sometimes cities.
I like plants to die.
I keep people from getting food.

I run out of power,
And stop smashing and bashing about,
And die down,
The sun, overpowering.

Christian Buckingham (9)
St Thomas More's Catholic Primary School, Colchester

Dragons!

Dragons are attacking,
They're flying everywhere,
Dragons are attacking,
Fire is in the air.

Dragons are attacking,
Everybody screams,
Dragons are attacking,
It's like a bad dream.

Dragons are attacking,
Everybody runs,
Dragons are attacking,
No one's having fun.

Dragons are attacking,
Lady Jane can give a hand,
Dragons are attacking,
She can save the land.

Dragons are attacking,
Time is running out,
Dragons are attacking,
Lady Jane then shouts!

Dragons are *not* attacking,
Our land has been saved,
Dragons are *not* attacking,
Thanks to Lady Jane!

Charlotte Hooper (8)
St Thomas More's Catholic Primary School, Colchester

My Horse

My horse's hooves dance in the paddock,
My horse's hooves swirl with me on top,
My horse's hooves clop when he trots,
My horse's hooves stand to attention,
My horse's hooves stand bolt upright,

My horse's mouth snaps when he is scared.

Kieran Smith (9)
St Thomas More's Catholic Primary School, Colchester

Snow

I make your Christmas fun and exciting,
I splatter myself in your garden,
I flood the streets with blizzards,
I freeze your windows,
I leave clothes drenched, not dry!
I make you wait in traffic
And crash your cars in the streets,
I rest, I'm melting,
People are coming out,
I'm feeling glum,
I think I'll rest here for the night!

Samara Allen-Mena (9)
St Thomas More's Catholic Primary School, Colchester

My Dog

My dog softly, comfortably licks your hand with his tongue,
His tongue is rough and tickly,
A pink and red soft tongue,
He rises on his hind legs when we bring food in,
My dog's legs crouch down ready to spring up at you to greet you,
His eyes gleam with cuteness and kindness,
His eyes are dark brown and it looks like he is always crying!

Roísín Clark (9)
St Thomas More's Catholic Primary School, Colchester

In The Big Bad Street

In the big bad street
Where the chavs all meet
And the grannies say, 'Get off my lawn!'
In the street big bad
Where the children play tag,
And the cows all say coo'koo!
In the bad big street
Where the houses are all sleek
And the cats all say ting!
Big bad street
Chavs all meet
Street big bad
Children play tag
Bad big street
Houses all sleek
What a horrible place to belong here!

Kirsty Davison (9)
Southbrook Junior School, Daventry

Untitled

There's more that goes to win a war
Than tanks and planes and guns
Than men prepared to do their best to overthrow evil ones.

Taylor Lee (10)
Southbrook Junior School, Daventry

There's Magic In The Air

There's magic in the air
I know I just can feel it
It's dancing through the air
Waiting for me to see it

The beautiful Northern Lghts
As they flicker in the night sky
Create for such a wonderful sight
Oh how I wish that I could fly

There's pink, red, orange and blue
Covering the night sky all the way through
There's magic in the air I can feel it
There's magic in the air, I am in it!

Eleanor Brightmore (10)
Southbrook Junior School, Daventry

My Sporty Poem

My best sport is speed stacks
beating the clock.
The next is netball
scoring a shot.
Hockey sticks click
in goes the ball.
Football is skills
tackle on pitches.
Cricket with a bat
get some runs.
Dancing and prancing
twirls and splits.

Elizabeth Bunce (11)
Thorpdene Junior School, Shoeburyness

Young Writers Information

We hope you have enjoyed reading this book - and that you will continue to enjoy it in the coming years.

If you like reading and writing poetry drop us a line, or give us a call, and we'll send you a free information pack.

Alternatively if you would like to order further copies of this book or any of our other titles, then please give us a call or log onto our website at www.youngwriters.co.uk

Young Writers Information
Remus House
Coltsfoot Drive
Peterborough
PE2 9JX

(01733) 890066